The Mountains Are The Story

A HISTORY OF TELLURIDE FOR CHILDREN

written by Duke Richey
illustrated by the children of Telluride Elementary School

First Edition

ISBN 0-9706361-0-5

Design and layout by SJS Design (Susan Smilanic)

Cover art by Fern Miller

Copies of this book can be ordered online at www.between-the-covers.com
or by calling Between the Covers Bookstore in Telluride, 970-728-4504

Between the Covers Bookstore
PO Box 2129
Telluride, CO 81435

A percentage of book sales revenue will be contributed to the Telluride Elemetary School Art Department.

For my godson John Lyons Brown, a genuine little mountain man.

This little book you hold in your hands has been in the works for enough years that I have forgotten whether it was even my idea originally to begin with or not. Chances are, it was not. Regardless, almost all of the credit for *The Mountains Are the Story* goes to my sister-in-law, Joanna Brown, who saw in this project an opportunity to envelop a number of her own true loves—children, art, books, education, and her beloved Telluride—into one beautiful and inclusive community project. Thank you, Joanna, for making this happen.

Thanks also to Abby Lia Collins Hamblin for being one of the best elementary school art teachers in America. The proof is in the pudding on every page of this book, Abby: You have helped unearth a motherlode of creativity in Telluride's wonderful young artists.

Thanks to Susan Smilanic for designing a charming finished product, for being enthusiastic from the start, and for guiding us through the process of turning a bunch of notes and rough drafts into a bedtime story people can actually pull off the shelf and read.

A big thanks to Michelle Kodis for lending a writer's eye to this story. It reads better because of your abilities and generosity.

Thank you, Sas, for proof-reading this and the hundreds of other less colorful things I will send your way in the future.

Most importantly, thank you to all the kids of Telluride. Whether you have a piece of art in this book or not, you can rest assured that you played a major role in shaping how this story was told. And the best part is you get to play a role in how the story will be told in the future. Love these mountains, kids, because they belong to you.

Duke Richey

Every place in the world has a story that goes with it. The stories explain the things that have happened there, including how the places were created and how they have changed and continue to change.

Stories about places are often about the things people have done and the things people do there. The United States, for example, has a different story than England. The U.S. has presidents, Coca-Cola, and baseball. England has royalty, tea, and cricket.

Just as countries are different, so are smaller places. The bathroom in your house is probably very different than the kitchen. Can you imagine doing things in the kitchen that you are supposed to do in the bathroom?

Or doing things in
the bathroom that you
are supposed to do in
the kitchen?

Since every place has a story, you should certainly know the story of your country, your hometown, and even the story of your house. You should know the story of your bedroom! Maybe someone famous used to live in your house, in your room, and you didn't even know it.

This book tells the tale of a place tucked away high in the San Juan Mountains of southwestern Colorado. It is a place with a colorful past and an astounding natural beauty. It is the story of a place called Telluride.

The mountains around Telluride were formed through complex processes over millions of years. Hot liquids deep in the planet's core bulged the earth's surface, then cooled to become hard rock mountains buried underground. Then, richly colored sands were deposited along the bulged surface by far-reaching oceans and blowing winds.

The red sandstone cliff bands above the town are proof that sandy beaches once covered Telluride.

Both the hard rock and the sandstone eventually buckled and fractured as the earth's landforms collided with one another. Later, snow-packed icy glaciers covered 1,900 miles of the San Juan Mountain area. The glaciers carried away large chunks of the mountains one inch at a time.

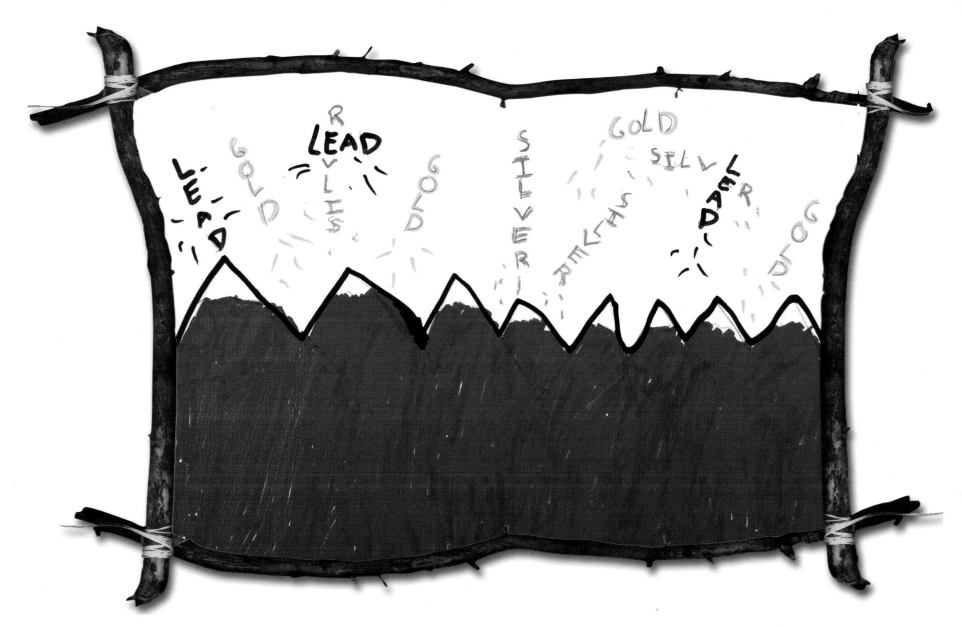

The two most amazing things about the mountain-building activity in the Telluride mountains are that the rocks were shot through with rich minerals like gold, silver, copper, and lead; and that the mountains were high enough to collect large amounts of snow.

The gold beneath the mountains, as well as the snow above it, created and continue to create stories that only mountains can tell. For this reason, in Telluride the mountains are the story.

Before there were skiers or festivals, and way before there were miners, the mountains were here and the only sounds were those of the wild. Elk bugled in the summer, eagles rustled in the cottonwood trees, and trout jumped in the river. In the winter, only the dampening whisper of falling snow could be heard.

One day a group of Ute Indians came here on a hunt, and they declared that the valley was the most beautiful they had ever seen. The Indians liked the fact that any animals they chased toward the waterfall had nowhere to hide. The end of the valley was a dead end. The Indians hunted, had great feasts, and enjoyed the aspen covered mountains rising all around them.

One day, when the Indians were away, a man from far away climbed over the mountains and saw the beautiful valley. The man was a Spaniard, who had travelled from Santa Fe, and he was in search of gold and silver. He looked in all the streams for sparkling yellow nuggets, but he left empty-handed. He had not seen what the mountains held in quiet abundance.

For many years the Indians had the mountains to themselves. Generations of Ute children grew up playing in the mountains and discovering their secrets.

One day in 1875, a man found a vein of gold and silver that had formed inside the mountains millions of years ago. He staked several claims on the land, all of which was owned by the United States government. He called his claims the Sheridan Mine and the Union Mine and by law the land around his claims eventually became his own. Before long the word was out: The mountains around the Ute valley were full of rich deposits.

Some men then discovered that the owners of the Sheridan and Union mines had made a mistake when surveying the size of their claims. They legally wedged their own mining claim between the Sheridan and Union. They called their mine the Smuggler because they had "smuggled" it into place between the two other mines.

Once miners began moving into the mountains near the Sheridan, Smuggler, and Union mines, there were bound to be some changes. As the newcomers put up their tents and built their wooden shacks, the Utes' sacred hunting ground gave way to a ramshackle village teeming with activity. The miners called their village Columbia.

Men came from all over the world to work in the mines. They had big dreams of hitting it rich. There were Swedes and Finns, Italians, Chinese, English, Germans, Irish, French, Welsh and Scots. Sometimes, there were so many different languages being spoken that no one could understand anything!

Soon Columbia was booming, and the people in the town tried to get the government to build a post office. The Columbians received word that they would have to come up with another name for their settlement because there was already another town called Columbia in California. The post office felt that this would lead to confusion since Columbia, CA, scrawled on the front of an envelope looked very much like Columbia, CO.

Eventually someone came up with the name Telluride. Some say it is a reference to an ore that is sometimes found in rock and has traces of gold and silver.

Between the founding of the Sheridan Mine and the end of the mining boom, there must have been many happy miners who found telluride in rocks above the town now known as Telluride. More than three hundred million dollars ($300,000,000) worth of minerals were mined from the mountains around the valley.

By the time the first train pulled into town in 1890, the people of Telluride had spent lots of money building their community. They constructed colorful houses, a strong brick hotel named after the original mine, a courthouse, a hospital, and a school. The Swedish and Finnish miners, many of whom moved around town on wooden skis, built their own meeting hall where they held dances and parties.

There were also many great feats of building and engineering in the mountains above town. Electricity generated by moving water provided power to run machinery, including the trams that miners used to get back and forth from home to work.

There were some things, though, that were not built for several years down the road. Before there were any churches, for example, preachers gave their sermons in saloons!

With the mountains turning out so much gold and silver, there was plenty of money in Telluride, and outlaws offered an occasional threat to the town's businesses. In 1889, Butch Cassidy and the Sundance Kid robbed the San Miguel County Bank of the entire monthly payroll for the town's miners.

In the early years of the 1900s, riches continued to pour forth from the mountains, and the town grew and prospered. In 1914, the famous Opera House adjoining the Sheridan Hotel was constructed just prior to a flood that covered much of the town in waist-deep mud.

After a few more years the mines began to shut down. The mountains had given all the gold and silver they could muster. As the miners moved away, leaving behind empty houses and closed down store fronts, the only people in the mines were occasional weekend adventurers. In the 1920s, some young men spent part of their summer sweeping enough gold dust off the floor of one mine that they were able to pay for college.

With the town nearly dead and mostly empty, the railroad quit sending a full-sized train to Telluride. In its place they sent the Galloping Goose, a train the size of a school bus. The Goose carried mail, supplies, and passengers into the mountains.

During World War II there was a great need for lead, zinc, and copper. Earlier, there was interest only in gold and silver, but with new demands for different minerals, mining in Telluride was reborn. Not long after the war ended, Telluride and the mountains surrounding it slipped back into a period of slow change. It was during these years that several local Telluridians had an idea. Some other old mining towns around the West had built ski areas where there had once been mines, so why couldn't it also be done in Telluride?

These local men put on heavy woolen pants and sweaters, then strapped on wooden skis using sturdy rubber bands to hold their boots to the boards. When the snow fell, they explored the mountains slopes with a dream of what their mostly empty town could become.

In the winter of 1970-71, the birth of the Telluride ski area took place before there were even any ski lifts in place. Snowcat machines shuttled skiers up and down the mountain.

Within a few years there were several ski lifts on the mountain, but skiers who skied all the way to town had to catch a bus back up to the top.

Word got out that the scenery and the skiing in the mountains around Telluride were magnificent, and young people from around the country began moving to the town to see what it had to offer.

What these newcomers found were picturesque mountains surrounding a town that had largely been abandoned. Empty houses and Main Street buildings could be bought for very little money and a lot of elbow grease.

Like the miners before them, these ski "pioneers" built and changed the mountain to fit their ideas and needs. They carved ski runs on the mountain's slopes and opened special businesses that catered to skiers.

They created summer festivals to attract crowds of tourists to Telluride once the snow melted. Where the first rope tow pulled skiers up a hill, thousands now watch worldclass hanggliders or musicians.

Where miners once enjoyed traveling entertainment shows, movie lovers now watch world premieres of films.

And on the mountain, where once there were the sounds of picks and shovels, dynamite, and the miner's song as men searched for gold and silver, people today explore the hills for fungi during the world-famous Telluride Mushroom Festival.

One can still see parts of the old Telluride today. Most of the buildings are still standing and Main Street looks much the same as it did one hundred years ago. A July 4th parade today differs only in that instead of a huge horse-drawn fire cart, Telluride now has a fire engine.

Instead of miners competing in rock-drilling contests, one may see skateboarders competing in Town Park. Surrounding all the activity are the mountains, which are much the same as they always were.

Just as the Utes discovered under the waterfalls, or the miners discovered with the first claims, today's skiers, hikers, bikers, and fishermen have come to realize that the story of the place we call Telluride is a story that has very much to do with what surrounds us. As it was to the people who came here hundreds of years ago, today the story of this place is a story of how the mountains and the town below have been used throughout history. Scarred and scoured, dug in and cut over, the mountains have retained their strength and majesty. The mountains stand over us, whispering that they will be here long after we are gone. Although things have changed and will continue to change, just as sure as new people move into and out of the area, it is still the case that the mountains are here and they are Telluride's story.